I will not wear your richly tattered cloak
I discard your taboo skirt
fashionable silence
fear of all I ask for
only what is fair
a simple testament to the dignity of my labour
all the joy of what I would not fear
the love of kings, of whores, of drunkards
of stars
the universe of my fingertips
my stubborn destiny
everything
in your face
the laughter
the dance
the sex
the unmistakable success
I make no excuse
the fire of my wit
stands
the glory of what can't be denied
you who omit me
a full third night
and the promise of my Fame.

~ from *Aphra*

Aphra

Nancy Jo Cullen
Alexandria Patience
Rose Scollard

In collaboration with Aphra Behn

 **Frontenac House**

Calgary, Alberta

Aphra was published as a 42-page chapbook by Playwrights Union of Canada Play Services, 1997.

Book and cover design: Epix Design
Cover images and other performance photographs: Frontenac House files.
Author photographs: Nancy Jo Cullen by Valeska San Martin;
Rose Scollard by E.V. Matthews

Library and Archives Canada Cataloguing in Publication

Cullen, Nancy Jo, author
    Aphra / Nancy Jo Cullen, Alexandria Patience, Rose Scollard.

A play.
Originally published: Toronto : PUC Play Service, 1997.
Issued in print and electronic formats.
ISBN 978-1-927823-45-3 (paperback).--ISBN 978-1-927823-46-0 (pdf).--ISBN 978-1-927823-47-7 (html)

    1. Behn, Aphra, 1640-1689--Drama. I. Patience, Alexandria, author II. Scollard, Rose, author III. Title.

PS8555.U473A64 2015   C812'.54   C2015-905973-9
                                               C2015-905974-7

We acknowledge the support of the Canada Council for the Arts for our publishing program. We also acknowledge The Alberta Media Fund for their support of our publishing program.

 Canada Council **Conseil des Arts**   *Alberta* Government
for the Arts du Canada

Printed and bound in Canada
Published by Frontenac House
1138 Frontenac Ave. SW
Calgary, Alberta, T2T 1B6, Canada
Tel: 403-245-8588
www.frontenachouse.com

For Aphra

All women together ought to let flowers fall upon the grave of
Aphra Behn ... for it was she who earned them the right to
speak their minds ... . Behn proved that money could be made
by writing at the sacrifice, perhaps, of certain agreeable
qualities; and so by degrees writing became not merely a sign of
folly and a distracted mind but was of practical importance.

~ Virginia Woolf, *A Room of One's Own*

Contents

Aphra

… that scurrilous, opinionated, lecherous, unimaginably wicked maker of plays — Aphra.

APHRA was produced by Maenad Theatre at the Pumphouse Theatres in Calgary, February 21 – March 9, 1991, with the following cast and crew:

Aphra, Boy, Stranger, Daring:	Nancy Jo Cullen
Betty Currer, Morality Man, Widow Ranter, Quack:	Alison Whitley
Mary Betterton, Morality Woman, Surelove, Quack's Assistant:	Catherine Myles
Director:	Alexandria Patience
Stage Manager:	Steph Kelemen
Lighting/Design:	Sandi Somers
Costumes:	Lizzie McGovern
Technician:	Howard Blake

Photos reproduced in this book are from the first production with Nancy Jo Cullen, Alison Whitley and Catherine Myles portraying their respective roles.

Aphra was re-mounted as part of the University of Calgary's Breaking the Surface Festival at the Pumphouse Theatre, Oct. 13 – Nov. 16,1991:

Aphra, Boy, Stranger, Daring:	Tanya Lukenoff
Betty Currer, Morality Man, Widow Ranter, Quack:	Alison Whitley
Mary Betterton, Morality Woman, Surelove, Quack's Assistant:	Catherine Myles
Director:	Alexandria Patience
Stage Manager:	Caroline Russell-King and Darcy Foggo
Lighting/Design:	Sandi Somers
Costumes:	Lizzie McGovern

Characters

Actor # 1	Aphra, Boy, Stranger, Daring
Actor #2	Betty Currer, Morality Man, Widow Ranter, Quack
Actor #3	Mary Betterton, Morality Woman, Surelove, Quack's Assistant

Setting

The setting is ephemeral and minimal with mood and place suggested by props and furnishings. Sometimes the action takes place in Aphra's rooms in seventeenth-century London. Sometimes it is adrift in time and space.

Act One

[*Lights up on* APHRA; *she is* en déshabillé, *beautiful in a worn kind of way, friendly and affable in manner. Holding a small candle in her hand, she addresses the audience.*]

APHRA: Good sweet honey-sugar-candied friends … which is more than anyone has called you yet. It used to be that these little addresses were made in rhyme but I understand that nowadays rhymes have been relegated to the nursery books. Even so, I will test your patience with one small couplet that was made about me after my death by an erstwhile lover. It was writ upon my grave and if you go to the Abbey you will find it there still. It reads:

> Here lies proof that wit can never be
> Defence enough against mortality.

This is of course a truism and could be written on the grave of any person of wit, past or present. But now with the hindsight of some three hundred years — I find it suits me well, except I would amend it. I would now have it read: "Here lies proof that wit can never be defence enough against … posterity."

There were many obstacles to playwriting in my day, not the least of which was poverty — Tom Otway, my dear friend and a gifted playwright, died of starvation and Wycherly was in debtors' prison for seven years and never wrote again because of it. But the biggest, chiefest enemy was that strange thing called moral opinion.

It was a two-fold creature, this moral opinion.

[*In the background* MORALITY MAN *steps out of the shadows. He wears a mask — a caricature of an old man, bearded and lascivious.*]

APHRA: On the one side it was decrepit, aged and moribund, clinging to life — like an old husband who would compel you to lie in the wide moth-eaten bed his forefathers lived and died in. An old husband you must kiss — nay, you must kiss none but him too, and nuzzle through his beard to find his lips and this you must submit to for all your three-score years.

[MORALITY WOMAN *in a veil and cloak moves prudishly from the shadows. She comes forward and joins* MORALITY MAN.]

APHRA: The other side of this morality was female. Yes, a woman. Upright, delicate of manner, so delicate that you would wonder at her impudence that would pretend to understand the thing called bawdy, she was the enemy of all that is natural, original or spontaneous. I understand you have such bonafide ladies even today.

[MORALITY MAN *and* WOMAN *dance a slow courtly measure.*]

APHRA: Together this elderly fool and this lady of delicate sensibility fought to save that artificial thing we call society, to preserve it from all intrusion of wit or novelty or imagination.

I battled with this two-fold monster all my life, and kept it at bay too. But after my death I am sad to tell you I was completely and utterly vanquished. I was not the only victim. They were chopping and changing old Will Shakespeare even in my lifetime and Otway was mutilated after death in a way I can hardly bear to relate.

I myself was consigned to oblivion. [*Goes to her desk and writes.*]

MAN: Intellectually, Mrs. Behn was qualified to lead the playwrights of her day through pure and bright ways.

WOMAN: But she was a mere harlot who danced through uncleanness and dared them to follow.

MAN: The wit of her comedies seems to be generally acknowledged.

WOMAN: And it is equally acknowledged that they are very indecent, on which account they ought not only to be held in the utmost detestation but cast into eternal oblivion.

MAN: Even if her life remained pure it is amply evident that her mind was tainted to the very core!

WOMAN: No one equalled this woman in downright nastiness.

[*They start out speaking the following lines but end in singing.*]

MAN: She's nasty!

WOMAN: She's lewd !

MAN: She's unclean!

WOMAN: She's bawdy!

MAN: She's rude!

WOMAN: She's obscene!

MAN: She's always déshabillé!

WOMAN: She's ruder than Rabelais!

MAN: And she *cracks* like a bawdy house queen!

WOMAN: She's a harlot.

MAN: She's a tart.

WOMAN: She's a whore.

MAN: She's a prude.

WOMAN: She's a bitch.

MAN: She's a bore.

WOMAN: Though she's loose in the bodice,

MAN: She's demure and she's modest

BOTH: as Nelly the Protestant Whore.

WOMAN: If you came expecting instruction and enlightenment, you may as well go home right now.

MAN: You obviously have nothing better to do with your time and money or you wouldn't be here.

WOMAN: You will no doubt be amused with what we have to show you. But don't be disarmed. Don't allow your good judgement to be clouded over. For you will realize, dear friends, to what baleful depths womankind can sink.

MAN: It is our intention to show you scenes from the life and dramas of that scurrilous, opinionated, lecherous, unimaginably wicked maker of plays — Aphra.

WOMAN: Behn.

MAN: Who was extravagantly,

WOMAN: Audaciously,

MAN: Quite unacceptably,

BOTH: *Alive!!*

MAN: She's nasty!

WOMAN: She's lewd!

MAN: She's unclean!

WOMAN: She's bawdy!

MAN: She's rude!

WOMAN: She's obscene!

MAN: She's always déshabillé,

WOMAN: She's ruder than Rabelais,

BOTH: And she *cracks* like a bawdy house queen!

WOMAN: We will begin where accounts of such lives should begin. At the end. Mrs. Behn is at her desk writing furiously. Her pen cannot keep up with her teeming brain.

MAN: She has been working like this for months.

WOMAN: Her publisher takes everything she writes but even so there is never enough income.

MAN: She has hopes of this last work, though. It is a play about the colonies. Working title: *Bacon in Virginia.* She thinks she might call it *The Widow Ranter.*

WOMAN: It's no masterpiece.

MAN: But it's witty, lucid and, like all her plays, extremely stageable. She's hoping a good third night will mend her broken fortunes.

WOMAN: That's how we pay our playwrights, from the proceeds of the third night.

MAN: Meanwhile she is cold, hungry, ill and in considerable pain.

WOMAN: It is April 14, 1689, two days before her death.

[MORALITY MAN *and* WOMAN *run off.* APHRA *writes feverishly.* MARY BETTERTON *comes in with a mug of chocolate. She fusses over* APHRA.]

MARY: I've arranged with Mrs. Bulker to light a little fire for you morning and evening. Only you must try to keep your shawl about you. And not sit in the draft of the window.

APHRA: Stop fussing with trifles, Mary. Tell me what Tom said.

[MARY *is silent for a while. Painfully so.*]

APHRA: What did he say, Mary? Will he do it?

MARY: I should go. You must rest.

APHRA: No, don't. You know I like my friends about me when I work. It's a warmth better than any fire or hot toddy.

MARY: Oh Aphra. [*She embraces* APHRA *tearfully.*]

[*Suddenly from below we hear cries and stomping feet of someone mounting the stairs.* BETTY CURRER *enters.*]

BETTY: Aphra! Aphra! Affy. Mary too. All the better. Look what I've brought. A little pie, some bread … and ale from Will's. My dear, how are you feeling?

APHRA: I feel wonderful.

BETTY: I've come to put some colour into this grey tub you live in. What shall we do, Mary? I know, you can bring us up to date on the *cackamerda* that passes for civilized living at His Majesty's Court.

MARY: There's no *cackamerda* in William's court. You should know that.

BETTY: How painfully true. They are all so terribly, terribly upright, William's bunch. God, I miss Charles. I even miss his stupid brother.

MARY: And Nelly.

APHRA: Sweet Nelly.

BETTY: I can't believe they're all dead.

APHRA: I must say you're doing a fine job of cheering me up.

BETTY: Dear God. Look, we'll have ale all round and we'll drink to our health.

[*All sing riotously "That Which I Dare Not Name".*]

> Down there we sat upon the moss
> And did begin to play
> A thousand amorous tricks to pass
> The heat of all the day.
> A many kisses did he give
> And I returned the same,
> Which made me willing to receive
> That which I dare not name,
> That which I dare not name.

BETTY: Now. What next? I know. Let's play questions and commands. You first, Mary.

MARY: Oh Betty, sit down. You're making me dizzy.

BETTY: I have it! We'll read the new play.

MARY: Betty. Not now.

BETTY: [*Picks up the script.*] *The Tragical History of Bacon in Virginia.* Why not now? Affy would love it, wouldn't you?

APHRA: I don't think it's quite Mary's kind of play.

BETTY: What? Mistress Surelove was made for Mary. Who else could play it to such delicate perfection. You have read the play ... [She looks puzzled.] Then what is it?

MARY: It's the widow, Betty.

BETTY: The widow is the best thing in it. I'm reading the widow, by the way. The play should be named for the widow.

APHRA: I have been thinking of it.

MARY: The Widow Ranter is ... improper.

BETTY: And when have we ever dealt in proper plays? I forgot, you're the paragon of virtue in the theatre world, aren't you, Mrs. B. [*Looks sly.*] But you haven't let that stop you from appearing in some pretty scurrilous productions.

MARY: But the widow's a departure, isn't she. With her britches I mean, and those manly ways.

BETTY: Women ape men on the stage all the time.

MARY: Indeed, but in other plays women pass as men for reasons of necessity or intrigue. The widow plays a man because ... she *likes* it.

BETTY: Does she now?

MARY: She is definitely a departure.

BETTY: But that's what's always so divine about Aphra's women — they're departures from the expected. Think of Julia, who keeps her lover. Think of Lady Knowell, who loves her books more than her wardrobe. And that great mound of dust Mistress Grimes, poor old Otway's landlady to the life, I always thought.

APHRA: Otway is dead four years today.

BETTY: Yes, I know. Dear Otway. That wonderful boy. But let's drink to his memory and be merry in the proper tradition of wakes.

MARY: Wakes!

BETTY: To Otway!

APHRA: To Otway.

BETTY: To Nell!

APHRA: To Nelly.

BETTY: To the Widow Ranter!

MARY: Betty, you're incorrigible!

BETTY: I love the widow! I want to be the widow! I'll make her as famous as I made Otway's Nicky Nacky. Come, we will read it. Let's do the part where Ranter visits Surelove. I'll be the widow. You will be simpery little Mrs. Surelove and you, Aphra, will be everybody else. [*They arrange themselves, ready to read the parts.*]

RANTER: How now, Boy. Is Madam Surelove at home?

BOY: Yes, Madam.

RANTER: Go tell her I am here, sirrah.

BOY: Who are you, pray forsooth?

RANTER: Why you son of a baboon, don't you know me?

BOY: No, Madam. I came over but in the last ship.

RANTER: What from Newgate or Bridewell? Go, ye dog, tell your lady the Widow Ranter is come to dine with her. Never mind, I see her. [*She moves over to* SURELOVE *and embraces her.*]

RANTER: My dear Jewel, how dost do? [*She waves off* BOY.] Here, boy, some pipes and a bowl of punch. [*To* SURELOVE] *You* know my humour, Madam, I must smoke and drink in the morning or I am mawkish all day.

SURELOVE: You drink punch in the morning?

RANTER: Punch! Tis my morning's draught, my table drink, my treat, my regalio, my everything! And my dear Surelove, if thou would but refresh and cheer thy heart with punch in a morning thou would not look thus cloudy all the day.

SURELOVE: I have reason, Madam, to be melancholy. I have received a letter from my husband in England who tells me the doctors can do no good on him. I fear I shall see him no more.

RANTER: Good news! I don't know how you put up with him for so long! An old fusty weather-beaten skeleton, as dried as stock fish and much of the hue. Come, come. Here's to the next. May he be young, Heaven I beseech thee.

SURELOVE: You have reason to praise an old man who died and left you worth fifty thousand pounds.

RANTER: Ay gad, and what's better, died in good time and left me young enough to spend his fifty thousand pounds in better company — rest his soul for that too.

SURELOVE: I doubt but t'will be all laid out on Lieutenant Daring.

RANTER: Faith I think I could lend it the rogue on good security.

SURELOVE: What's that? To be bound body for body?

RANTER: Rather that he should love no body's body besides my own. But my fortune is too good to trust the rogue. My money makes me skeptical of men.

SURELOVE: You think they all love you for your money?

RANTER: For that, ay, what else? If it were not for that, I might sit still and sigh, and cry out, a Miracle! a Miracle! at sight of a man within my doors.

BOY: A gentleman is without.

RANTER: It's not Daring, that rogue, is it?

BOY: No, madam.

RANTER: Is he handsome? Does he look like a gentleman?

BOY: He's handsome. And seems a gentleman.

RANTER: Send him in, then. I hate a conversation without a fellow. [BOY *exits and* STRANGER/APHRA *enters, who carries a letter for* MARY.]

RANTER: Hah! A good handsome fellow indeed !

SURELOVE: With me, sir, would you speak?

STRANGER: If you are Madam Surelove.

SURELOVE: So I am called.

STRANGER: Madam, I am newly arrived from England, and from your husband my kinsman bring you this. [*Hands over a letter.*]

RANTER: Please do you sit, sir. Will you smoke a pipe?

STRANGER: [*Sitting beside* SURELOVE *and clasping his cane manfully between his knees*] I never do, Madam.

RANTER: O fie upon it, you must learn then. We all smoke here. 'Tis a part of good breeding. Well well, what cargo, what goods have ye? Any points, lace, rich stuffs, jewels? If you have, I'll be your retailer. I live hard by. Anybody will direct you to the Widow Ranter's.

STRANGER: I have already heard of you, Madam.

RANTER: What! You are like all the young fellows. The first thing they do when they come to a strange place is to enquire what fortunes there are. [*She sits beside him and places her hand suggestively on the cane above his.*]

STRANGER: Madam, I had no such ambition. [*He places his other hand above and close to hers.*]

RANTER: Gad, then you're a fool, sir. We rich widows are the best commodity this country affords, I'll tell you that. [*Her hand reaches out to top the cane but* SURELOVE *beats her to it. They laugh together, enjoying the moment, but* APHRA *slumps forward, somewhat overcome.*]

MARY: Affy! Are you ill?

APHRA: Just a little heated. But don't stop, I'm enjoying it.

BETTY: It's a treat, Aphra. A masterpiece. Mary, you make an adorable Surelove. The part was writ for you. And Tom will be perfect as Hazard. As for me … Bill Smith as my General Daring. I rather fancy having a go at Bill with my poignard. When is the opening planned for? [*Pointed silence from* MARY]

APHRA: There aren't any plans at the moment.

BETTY: Well, what's the delay? It's finished, isn't it. [*She interprets the silence.*] I might have known. So what is it this time? Jealousy? He's afraid Bill's Daring will eclipse his Hazard?

MARY: Tom is incapable of jealousy.

BETTY: Or maybe it's politics. The play might offend someone on either side of the fence he perches on?

MARY: Stuff!

BETTY: We all know your precious husband won't touch anything with political innuendo.

MARY: Tom believes that the stage is not the proper place to air political views.

BETTY: What harm is there in this poor play, apart from the proposal that those who run things are fools and charlatans.

MARY: It's more a question of good taste than politics.

BETTY: Good what? Ah, we're getting back to the widow, are we? You don't like her swaggering ways?

MARY: Well really, Betty. All that drinking and smoking.

BETTY: And all that initiative.

MARY: Exactly. It's most unseemly.

BETTY: Oh God. Tighten your stays and button your lips. There's a bonafide woman in the house.

MARY: I just don't think it's proper to have the widow playing suitor.

BETTY: So a woman putting on britches as an excuse to show her legs is acceptable but putting them on as a show of strength is not?

MARY: What drivel you spout, Betty.

BETTY: And yet it's for this very drivel you abandon your friend when she needs you.

MARY: That's not true. Why I …

BETTY: Because she refuses to put virtue before zest in her women.

MARY: Tom thinks women on the stage have enough trouble protecting their good name …

BETTY: Tom's an arse licker and you're a prig.

MARY: Oh really. Well, you play any sort of scum.

APHRA: [*Happily observing the struggle*] Isn't it wonderful? I am so greedy of my cabal's time and affection that I find the most inspiration for writing while in their lively midst, taking questions, phrases and disagreements as a lucky chance to move my quill in new directions. I choose to write, and I choose not to hide away from life and love's gay goings-on but to etch my words while in the middle of the maelstrom and not as a nun secluded and secure from trade winds. Lately, I am haunted by all manner of dreams and ideas and much of my past rises up before me and presents itself as if I were at the Theatre Royal, passing a pleasant evening with friends, seeing the latest effort of Otway or Etheridge. Behind me are my friends, a gay rabble gathered together not to roar but certainly to rant a little, tantivy and merry. Laughter and tuberose and teasing surround me. But some of those I glimpse could not in any way be termed my intimates, though some would wish to claim it. And one, or maybe two, I would. But let's journey a little towards friendship and understanding before we share our secrets of love and loves.

[*As* APHRA *speaks,* MARY *and* BETTY, *squabbling, transform into the moral monster* MORALITY MAN *and* MORALITY WOMAN.]

WOMAN: That's enough of that, now.

APHRA: Enough of what?

WOMAN: Enough of that endless babble. Women should be seen and not heard. [WOMAN *puts hand over* APHRA'S *mouth.*] Am I right, my Lord?

MAN: Absolutely. And they should be obscene and not heard, too. [MAN *reaches round and cups* APHRA'S *breast, jiggling it a little.*]

WOMAN: If they know what's good for them. Poor thing, she's trying to say something. She'll never learn. They say when you're close to death that the events of your life pass before you — a kind of review of the thing before you let it go.

MAN: That's how it was for our fair Aphra those last days. When she wasn't in a turmoil of work she was in a turmoil of memories, some real, some not so real.

WOMAN: I don't know what it was that caused her delirium.

MAN: It could have been drink. Some said she had a sciatic condition, a sort of rheumatism.

WOMAN: It was probably the pox.

MAN: In her fever she saw herself as though she was on stage, played by Betty and Mary. The two warring factions in her …

WOMAN: The demure and beautiful …

MAN: The wicked and daring.

WOMAN: Sometimes she seemed to be one …

MAN: Sometimes the other.

WOMAN: Sometimes they didn't seem like Betty and Mary at all but more like that moral monster she dreaded. All the stepping stones of her life were there, not spread out in a clean line across the stream, but confused and out of order, moving back and forth across a raging torrent it seemed she would never cross.

MAN: Why look at this! There are little wounds appearing all over her body.

WOMAN: Stigmata?

MAN: No. Paper cuts. She's lacerated with cuts that slice into her body. And each wound is splitting open to show different things. [MAN *and* WOMAN *examine* APHRA *closely.*]

WOMAN: Like an advent calendar. [*Looks at* APHRA'S *wrist.*] Yes, you can get a pretty good idea of what she's been up to,

I choose to write, and I choose not to hide away from life and love's gay goings-on but to etch my words while in the middle of the maelstrom and not as a nun secluded and secure from trade winds.

looking at these. Politics. Intrigue. Eugh! Not a womanly sort of life at all.

MAN: Love. There's lots of that. Aphra and her lovers. Etheredge, Rochester, John Boyes, Otway.

WOMAN: Now, you don't know that.

MAN: Here's the day she first saw John Hoyle. I can just make out what it says: "Your body easy and all tempting lay." I never understood what she saw in him. The man's an infidel.

WOMAN: [*Forgetting herself*] But such an agreeable infidel. [*She gets a nasty look from* MAN *and looks demure again.*]

WOMAN: Why, here's opening night of *The Rover.*

MAN: And here's where she found her first grey hair. And look! Here's where she was born.

WOMAN: Are you sure?

MAN: Yes. Why?

WOMAN: Well I've heard it said that she never was born, that she never really existed.

APHRA: I was so born. And baptized too.

MAN: But do you have the paper to prove it?

APHRA: The record's in the parish register. It must be there.

MAN: It must be. Of course.

APHRA: Everyone has to come in the world the same way.

MAN: There is only one way. [WOMAN *groans and sits down breathing heavily.* MAN *goes behind her and emerges between her legs. He is now* YOUNG APHRA.]

WOMAN: What is it? A boy or a girl?

APHRA: A girl of course.

WOMAN: She hurt enough for a boy. Kicking and lunging like that.

MAN: [*As* YOUNG APHRA] Why not? I mean to be a hero.

WOMAN: But you're a gentlewoman, a lady.

YOUNG APHRA: Does this mean I can't have fun?

WOMAN: As your mother I must instruct you how a married woman of your quality ought to live.

YOUNG APHRA: Married? But I'm just a baby.

WOMAN: Beginning at eight and ending before twelve you ought to employ yourself in dressing.

YOUNG APHRA: Four hours to dress?

WOMAN: Till two at dinner. Till five in visits. Till seven at the theatre. Till nine walking in the park. Ten, supper with your husband.

APHRA: Or with your lover if your husband be not home.

WOMAN: Fie! Don't put ideas in her head.

APHRA: From ten to twelve are the happy hours, the *Bergère*, those of entire enjoyment.

YOUNG APHRA: And what must I do from twelve till eight again?

APHRA: Oh, those are the dull conjugal hours for sleeping with your own husband and dreaming of joys your absent lover alone can give.

YOUNG APHRA: And that's it? Is there nothing more to a woman's life than that?

WOMAN: What more could you want?

YOUNG APHRA: I want to travel to the four corners of the earth. I want to have adventures. To be a sailor or a spy. I want to learn things, to understand the workings of the heavens and all manner of things. I want to learn Greek and Latin and write plays as good as Ben Jonson's.

WOMAN: You poor fool. Do you really imagine a woman can do those things? A woman must be seen and not heard. [YOUNG APHRA *mouths the words "seen and not heard".*] A spy! The idea!

MAN: [*Once again* MAN *looks at* APHRA'S *shoulder and reads a wound.*] So dark. So mysterious.

WOMAN: It's a letter.

MAN: Antwerp, Belgium.

WOMAN: This 27th Day of August, Sixteen Hundred and Sixty-Six:

APHRA: My Lord Killigrew, need I tell you that as of yet Halsall has not replied to my letters and I am most pressed for money. This country is so expensive that I must spend 10 guilders a day simply to maintain a respectable appearance of life. As I cannot go to Holland for fear that English refugees will betray me, I have had to send Celadon the money to make two journeys to me, each of which cost me 10 pounds. The 40 pounds I brought with me have been spent ...

MAN: Spying in the king's honour.

WOMAN: A lady would do no such thing.

MAN: Only a lady could complete such a task.

WOMAN: [*Disgusted*] Feminine wiles.

MAN: Which earlier you suggested would be the only talents she could acquire. [*Pause while she watches* APHRA] And still she is left without support to fend for her life.

APHRA: My lord Arlington, I must call on your better feelings. I know the justness of the cause in which I am engaged. Otherwise I would be wild at my hard treatment.

MAN: But the plague rages through London. What does she expect?

WOMAN: Yes, and the king and his party flee to the countryside.

MAN: I hear tell the "king's friends" in the Netherlands complain of their scanty rewards. They are easily forgotten such a distance from home.

APHRA: You are my last hope and the fountain of mercy. The delays in sending money have caused me to incur twice the expenses I would otherwise have had. I need a bill for one hundred pounds. Without this I cannot even return. I am a poor stranger and my life depends on receiving the money. I will remind you that I desired neither the place nor the voyage. I must return on the next convoy or I will have to wait another two months.

MAN: How did you get home?

APHRA: I would not beg or starve and so I had to obtain credit.

WOMAN: The London to which you return has been rendered unbearable by the Great Fire.

MAN: [*Sings with* WOMAN *as a round.*] London's burning, London's burning !

WOMAN: Bring the water! Bring the water!

MAN: Fire! Fire!

WOMAN: Fire! Fire!

APHRA: Acres of ruins and sights more strange than the jungles of Surinam. Nor can I recall such cold. The Thames is frozen over.

MAN: [*Sings.*] When will you pay me, said the bells of Old Bailey.

WOMAN: [*Sings.*] When will you pay me?

MAN: [*Sings.*] When will you pay me?

APHRA: When they pay *me*.

WOMAN: Parliament keeps a tight rein on the king's coffers. His money, they believe, is poorly enough spent on his mistresses.

MAN: The government has lost its yield of the chimney tax. And the destruction by fire of the merchandise warehouses has lost us months' worth of trade and our valuable war stores.

WOMAN: Yet the fire has extinguished the plague. For that we rejoice …

APHRA: When they pay me!

WOMAN: But your creditors are unwilling to meet the slow pleasure of the court.

APHRA: Sir, if you could guess at the affliction of my soul you would I am sure pity me. Tis tomorrow that I must submit myself to a prison, the time being expired. And though I endeavored all day yesterday to get a few days more, I cannot, because they say I am dallied with all and so they say I shall be forever. So I cannot revoke my doom and I have cried myself dead, and could find in my heart to break through all this to get to the king and never rise till he were pleased to pay this. But I am sick and weak and unfit for it, or a prison. I shall go tomorrow. But I will send my mother to the king with a petition, for I see that everybody is only words and I will not perish in a prison from whence Butler swears I shall not stir until the utmost farthing be paid, and oh God, who considers my misery and my charge too, this is my reward for all my endeavors. Sir, if I have not the money tonight you must send me something to keep in prison, for I will not starve.

WOMAN: Oh, look at this one. [*Examines wound on* APHRA'S *thigh.*] Beautiful. Exotic.

MAN: It's lovely. This must be when she travelled to the Americas. To Surinam.

APHRA: It was the loveliest place on earth. Groves of oranges, lemons, citrons, figs, nutmegs. The people there, the natives, their lives were so simple and so wise. They didn't need our laws, our religion. They lived according to their nature.

WOMAN: No laws!

MAN: No religion !

WOMAN: But how did they deal with crime?

APHRA: They had their own justice.

MAN: And sin?

WOMAN: Yes.

MAN: And who was the overseer of their labour?

WOMAN: How did the work get done?

APHRA: Toil and sin, that's what the white man's gifts are.

[MAN *and* WOMAN *softly chant "toil and sin" throughout the rest of* APHRA's *speech.*]

APHRA: First, he loads you down heavier than any beast of burden. Then he beats you for your sins. And this misfortune is worse than fire. Fire lasts but a day or two. Or plague. Plague is over in a matter of months. But slavery is forever. It has no foreseeable end.

WOMAN and MAN: There will be no end to their misfortunes!

APHRA: And no end to mine. I too am doomed to eternal slavery. Bound in silence. Bound in silence. Sewn up.

WOMAN and MAN: Poor little Aphra, all sewn up.

WOMAN: I have heard tell of a tribe where if a woman is found talking too loud or for too long or of things she ought not to, they have a very swift and obvious punishment: her tongue is ripped from her, her lips are sewn shut. Or she is stoned to silence.

MAN: Now let's be honest, my sweet fellow charmer, mmm? Think about this. Would a certain one of us here still be firmly attached to her tongue? It would have fed the fishes long ago.

WOMAN: And those noisy fingers would have been thrown to the dogs. And those noisy eyes would have been a treat for the cat.

MAN: Still too noisy! Sewn up and finally stoned. Silence … silence …

APHRA: It's true. I'm already sewn up. This matter of oblivion has been concerning me for some time. No matter how fast I write there is someone faster to erase it. When I'm dead …

WOMAN: [*Becoming* MARY *again*] Dead? What kind of talk is that!

APHRA: No one will remember me. No one will read my books. They will forget about me.

MARY: You should be resting. How can you possibly get better if you don't nurse yourself.

APHRA: I have to finish. I have to get it all down!

MARY: But you're in pain.

APHRA: It's nothing. Nothing to the pain of oblivion.

MAN: [*Is* BETTY *again*] You'll fight it, Affy. The way you've always fought to be heard.

APHRA: I can't fight it if I'm dead.

BETTY: If anyone will, you will.

MARY: You're like ice. Should we send for Dr. Kenney?

BETTY: Let's see how she does.

APHRA: [*Writing furiously*] I won't be stopped. Not now or ever.

[BETTY *and* MARY *shift back into* MORALITY MAN *and* WOMAN *and comment on* APHRA *as she writes feverishly. She is beleaguered and threatened but undaunted.*]

WOMAN: No one equalled her in downright nastiness.

MAN: She dances through uncleanness.

WOMAN: A disgrace to her sex and to the language.

APHRA: What is my crime after all? All I ask is the privilege for my masculine part, the poet in me.

MAN: You blasphemed the sacred temple Marriage.

APHRA: Marriage is as certain a bane to love as lending money is to friendship.

WOMAN: Your plays are lewd and wicked.

APHRA: That is the most unjust and silly aspersion woman could invent to pass on woman — that it is *bawdy* — the least and most excusable fault in the men writers to whose plays you all crowd. But from a woman it is unnatural.

MAN: *The City Heiress, Sir Patient Fancy*, both disgusting!

WOMAN: *The Lucky Chance.*

APHRA: The play had no other misfortune but that of coming out for a woman's. Had it been owned by a man, though the most dull, unthinking, rascally scribbler in town, it had been a most admirable play.

MAN: A woman belongs in the home, not in the market place.

APHRA: I'm forced to write for bread and not ashamed to own it.

WOMAN: Your life is scarcely exemplary. All those *lovers.*

APHRA: I wish only that there had been more. Who can be

happy without love? For me, I never numbered those dull days amongst those of my life in which I had not my soul filled with that soft passion.

MAN: You're altogether too lippy.

APHRA: I despise the malicious world that will allow a woman no wit.

WOMAN: You write in extremes!

APHRA: All my life is nothing but extremes.

[APHRA *shows signs of breakdown and succumbing to her delirium.* MORALITY MAN *and* WOMAN *change to* QUACK *and his* ASSISTANT.]

APHRA: I must have the doctor.

ASSISTANT: Why you are in luck, Madam. This man is a doctor, and as eloquent a doctor, Madam, as ever put a bill in the post.

QUACK: Pray let me feel your pulse, Madam.

APHRA: You seem most familiar to me.

ASSISTANT: What think you, Doctor, is she not very far gone?

QUACK: Far. Far. Tell me, Madam. Have you not a certain wambling pain in your stomach?

APHRA: The pain is in my shoulders and …

QUACK: I knew it by her stinking breath. [*To* ASSISTANT, *who nods wisely*] And are you not troubled with a pain in your head?

APHRA: In my head, sir, yes.

QUACK: Ahah! And a kind of vertigo as the Latins call it, or a whirligigoustiphon, as the Greeks have it, which signifies in English, Madam, a dizzy swimming kind of a — do ye see — a thing that — a — you understand me?

I despise the malicious world that will allow a woman no wit.

APHRA: Indeed yes. [*Holding her head*] How did you know?

ASSISTANT: This is a rare man!

QUACK: Well, Madam, Haley the Moor and Rabbi Isaac and some thousands of the more learned Dutchmen have found your crossed eyes and your whirligigoustiphon to be inseparable.

ASSISTANT: A most learned reason. What do you think her chances are?

QUACK: I think her case is desperate. But! We shall soon rectify the quiblets and quillities of her blood, if she observes our directions and diet, which is to eat but once in four or five days.

APHRA: In other words, you prescribe starvation. You must have doctored Otway.

QUACK: [*Sulking*] Unless she follows our prescription she's a dead woman.

ASSISTANT: Copy this down! [APHRA *takes up her quill and writes, as* QUACK *rapidly dictates.* ASSISTANT *doses her as she writes.*]

QUACK: Every morning, a dose of my pills Merda Quorusticon. Every hour, six score drops of Aminicula Vitae. At night, twelve cordial pills Gallimofritucus. Let blood once a week, and a glister once a day. After her sleep, threescore restorative pills called Cheatus Redivivus. And lastly, fifteen spoonfuls of liquid Belladonna … [ASSISTANT *pours the liquid into* APHRA'S *mouth.*]

QUACK: To be dropped into the eyes, as often as necessary.

ASSISTANT: The *eyes*?

QUACK: Of course the eyes. Taken internally it's a deadly poison!

ASSISTANT: Oops!

QUACK: Well. That's the end of her.

APHRA: The end?

ASSISTANT: Hmm. You won't be needing this anymore. [*Takes away her quill.*]

QUACK: We win, my pretty one. You belong to me now. [*He makes nasty advances to her.*]

APHRA: Prithee sir, leave off being an old buffoon! Who wants a lover turned ridiculous by age. Look at yourself! Your face is like an old worm-eaten cheese.

QUACK: Well, widow, you do like your little joke.

ASSISTANT: She's pure company. Ha ha.

QUACK: But whatever my countenance, I win. You're dead and in my power at last.

APHRA: No! Never! I'll never yield! [*Struggle ensues. At first the figures struggle with her and berate her. Then they turn into* BETTY *and* MARY *trying to soothe and calm her.*]

ASSISTANT: Harlot!

QUACK: Bitch!

APHRA: No! Give me that pen.

MARY: Aphra! Calm yourself!

BETTY: Affy. Affy! Don't you know me?

APHRA: Betty? Oh Betty!

MARY: Here, sit you down. We brought you a posset from Dr. Kenney.

APHRA: No doctors, I pray you!

MARY: Drink. It will make you feel better.

BETTY: You should be in bed.

APHRA: No. There is so much to do. I'll write till the light goes, at least. Did you speak to Tom?

MARY: Well …

BETTY: [*Interrupting*] I did. And he's all for it.

APHRA: He is? Truly?

MARY: I …

BETTY: Truly! He thinks it's a wonderful play. Said Mary had completely misunderstood him and he'd love to play the part of Hazard. And Mary's to play Surelove and I the Widow herself.

APHRA: Wonderful. That's truly wonderful. The play is bound to succeed.

BETTY: It can't fail.

MARY: [*Aside*] She won't thank you for lying to her.

BETTY: [*Looking at* APHRA *feverishly writing*] I don't think she'll be with us long enough to know I did.

MARY: Oh Betty! [*They embrace.* MARY *turns her head to audience and is suddenly* MORALITY WOMAN.]

WOMAN: Betty was right. It was over for Mistress Behn. But she worked to the last, turning out her scurrilous work. She touched up her play too, happy in the thought that it would be produced by Betterton and would give some fame to that worthless creation the Widow Ranter. More of that wretched misfit later. [BETTY, *still in* MORALITY WOMAN'S *embrace, turns her face and is now* MORALITY MAN.]

MAN: For now, we will leave Aphra with her burning pen and her blurring eyes. And, given her complexion and her condition, we won't be too harsh on her.

> Long with a sciatica, she's besides lame,
> Her limbs distortured, nerves shrunk up with pain.

And therefore I'll all sharp reflections shun
Poverty, Poetry, Pox are plagues enough for one.

[MORALITY MAN *kisses* MORALITY WOMAN, *then lasciviously
follows her off.* APHRA *writes on.*]

Sir, you fight for one that loves you not.

Act Two

[APHRA, *cloaked, holding a candle, enters in the dim light and addresses the audience.*]

APHRA: Dear friends. Forgive me for drifting in and out of your view like this. And bear with me a little longer; there's not much more to say. Towards the end of my life, it was hard not to let depressions come. If it had not been for the ministrations of my friends I would surely have foundered. But they kept me warm and tended me, shored me up with love. I rejoiced in their company, especially the young people, of whom there were a great number. Right up to the end there was always a new crop of young writers thronging about me. Occasionally, though, my fears did emerge. After all it was obvious I was on the way out. I wrote furiously and acquitted myself well. Some works from that time I am not unhappy with. My novels, some of the translations, there was even a play or two. *The Lucky Chance,* now there was a play I was fond of. A good piece of work and if it was too lively for some tastes, it suited others well. They tried to censor it, of course. But you would find nothing offensive in it, unless you are offended by the idea that marriage is a sham. I'm sure, though, that it sealed my fate as far as moral opinion was concerned. I was forever after seen as that lascivious creature, dancing through indecency and uncleanness. And all my stagecraft, all my truthfulness of character, all my cleverness with intrigue and plotting went for nought. I was cast adrift to float in that great sea of anonymity. *The Widow Ranter?* It was produced at the urgings of Betty and one or two of my young writers, one year after my death.

[*Lights up on* BETTY, *dressing*]

APHRA: Here's Betty now in the tiring room of the Duke's Theatre putting on her britches for the second act. She's in a foul mood. The play is not going well. It's a disaster! But you'll hear enough about that from Betty herself. It's well beyond my care or my help. As I feared — nay, as I predicted — I have been abandoned. My friends Otway, Congreve, Wycherly, they all have taken their places in the halls of fame, as well they should have. But I ...

> The breeze that wafts the crowding nations o'er,
> Leaves me unpitied far behind
> On the forsaken barren shore
> To sigh with Echo, and the murmuring wind.
> Thus while the chosen seed possess the promised land,
> I, like the excluded prophet, stand;
> The fruitful happy soil can only see,
> But am forbid by fate's decree
> To share the triumph of the joyful victory.

[APHRA *sits beside* BETTY, *who, muttering and cursing under her breath, adjusts her clothing.* MARY *enters.*]

BETTY: Oh. It's you.

MARY: I came to wish you well, Betty.

BETTY: Wish me well? If you wished me well, you'd be here beside me.

MARY: Well, Tom didn't think ...

BETTY: If you couldn't do it for me couldn't you have done it for Aphra? She was your friend, wasn't she?

MARY: Of course she was. And we did our best for her, too. We got her into the Abbey, didn't we? Tom had to go to no end of trouble. But she's there for ever and ever.

BETTY: But not in Poets' Corner where she belongs.

MARY: Well, only the greatest are there, Betty.

BETTY: Only the men are there.

MARY: Here, let me help you with that. [*Fixes her lace.*]

BETTY: I don't know why I'm fussing so much. It won't do a bit of good. The play's a complete bungle. They murdered it, Mary. They dropped whole scenes from it. It's the Whig faction behind it, I'm convinced. And Daring. Did you see the poor snivelling wretch they got for him? I can't believe Tom couldn't have done something to help. Was it the Whig faction, Mary?

MARY: I'm sure I wouldn't know that.

BETTY: Or was it the bonafide ladies!

MARY: I hope you don't think I had anything to do with it.

BETTY: Here I am about to play this torrid scene with … Samuel Sanford. A man better suited to playing Caliban. He's round shouldered, meagre face, spindled-shanked, splay footed. It's the worst casting job in the history of the Duke's.

MARY: Jenkins has done well by the play. Dryden himself provided the prologue, did he not?

BETTY: The producers mangled it. The play doesn't have a chance. The best play that was ever writ wouldn't have a chance if it had the fate to be murdered like this. The casting is lamentable, the acting execrable. Everyone is determined to ruin Aphra in her grave. If Aphra were alive she would have committed it to the flames rather than have suffered it to be presented thus. I put it down to politics. The play has offended someone.

MARY: Really, Betty. Must you go on like this?

BETTY: But maybe the Widow Ranter is too strong a character for them to stomach. As long as we're bawdy then dressing as men is tolerated, but the widow is just too feisty and overbearing. Well, I'll show them. I'll drive those ninnies from the audience with the performance I intend to give. That includes you, Mistress Betterton.

MARY: Betty. Let's not part in anger. Think of all the good times we had. Can there be no more good times … for Aphra's sake? I know you're angry, but think of the fun we had. The games. The gatherings. The songs.

[BETTY *is softening but sulks on as* MARY *cajoles.*]

MARY: Remember when George was courting Annie and we put the sleeping draft in his ale? Remember when Bill put the dried dog poo in Rochester's snuff? Remember when Gerry was foutering the orange girl in the back of the tiring room and we stole all his clothes? Remember the times we had, the ale we drank, and all the songs we sang. [*Sings softly*] "That which I dare not name, That which I dare not name." [*Then sings the following.*]

> Amyntas led me to a grove
> Where all the trees did shade us;
> The sun itself though it had strove
> It could not have betrayed us.
> The place secured from human eye
> No other fear allows,
> But when the winds that gently rise
> Do kiss the yielding boughs,
> Do kiss the yielding boughs.

BETTY and MARY:

> Down there we sat upon the moss
> And did begin to play
> A thouand amorous tricks to pass
> The heat of all the day.
> A many kisses did he give
> And I returned the same,
> Which made me willing to receive
> That which I dare not name,
> That which I dare not name.

MARY:

> His charming eyes no aid required
> To tell the softening tale;
> On her that was already fired
> 'Twas easy to prevail.

BETTY:

> He did but kiss and clasp me round
> Whilst those his thoughts expressed
> And laid me gently on the ground
> Ah, who can guess the rest,

TOGETHER:

> Ah, who can guess the rest.

[*While they sing,* APHRA *joins in. Then she rises and goes off stage and discards cloak. She returns masked and in britches, whistling the tune of the song in a sprightly manner.*]

BETTY: Who's that? Tom? Come to wish me well like Mary, you old hypocrite? No, it's Bill. So Tom let you come, did he? What, shall we run through it? Give it our best? [BETTY *and* APHRA *take on the roles of* RANTER *and* DARING. *Later,* MARY *becomes* SURELOVE.]

RANTER: Look now, this damned mad fellow Daring, who has my heart and soul, loves Surelove and has stolen her and carried her away to his tent. She hates him, while I am dying for him.

[*To herself*] Dying, Madam? When was the Widow Ranter ever melancholy?

Pox on it, no. Why should I sigh and whine and make myself an ass. No! Instead of snivelling I am resolved … [*Clasps her sword.*] Gad ! To beat the rascal and cart off Surelove. [*Approaches masked figure.*]

RANTER: Can you direct me, sir, to one Daring's tent.

DARING: One Daring! He has another epithet to his name!

RANTER: What's that? Rascal? Or coward?

DARING: Hah! Which of thy stars, young man, has sent thee hither to find that certain fate they have decreed?

RANTER: I know not what my stars have decreed. I shall be glad if they have ordained me to fight with Daring. By thy concern thou shouldst be he.

DARING: I am. Prithee, who art thou?

RANTER: Thy rival, newly arrived from England, and come to marry fair Surelove, whom thou has carried off. You carried off the wrong one, I fancy, for I hear another lady dies for you.

DARING: Dies for me?

RANTER: Therefore resign her — or fight me fairly.

DARING: Come on, sir — but hold — before I kill thee, prithee inform me who this dying lady is?

RANTER: Sir, I owe ye no courtesy and therefore will do you none by telling you — come sir, for Surelove — draw!

DARING: Draw!

RANTER: Sir, you fight for one that loves you not.

DARING: Perhaps she'll love you as little.

RANTER: Gad, put it to the trial, if you dare. Bring me to her and whom she does neglect shall give the other place.

DARING: That's fair. Put up thy sword. I'll bring thee to her instantly. Madam!

[MARY *steps forward.*]

DARING: The complaisance I show in bringing you my rival will let you see how glad I am to oblige you every way.

RANTER: I hope the danger I have exposed myself to for the honour of kissing your hand, Madam, will render me something acceptable.

SURELOVE: Ranter?

RANTER: [*Clasping her hand and drawing her aside*] Dear Creature, I have taken this habit to free you from an impertinent lover and to secure this damn rogue Daring to myself. He thinks I am your cousin. Play along with me.

SURELOVE: Dear cousin, receive my welcome.

RANTER: Stand by, General. [*Pushes* DARING *away, looks big and takes* SURELOVE *by the hand and kisses it.*]

DARING: [*Angry at being pushed*] 'Sdeath sir!

[RANTER *draws her sword.*]

SURELOVE: Ranter! I mean Cousin. You can't mean to fight him.

RANTER: And beat him too.

SURELOVE: [*Drawing her aside*] What? A woman beat a lieutenant general?

RANTER: Hang 'em! They get a name in war from command, not courage.

SURELOVE: But if he should kill you …

RANTER: I'll take care to make it as comical a duel as the best of them. As much in love as I am, I do not intend to die its martyr.

DARING: Nay sir, I'll not fight.

RANTER: Then you yield the prize?

DARING: Ay Gad, since she prefers such a callow fop as thou before a man. Take her and domineer. Death, I am grown ridiculous.

RANTER: Faith sir, if I were you I would devote myself to Madame Ranter. She's the fittest wife for you. She'll fit your humour.

DARING: Ranter! Gad, I'd sooner marry a she-bear, unless for a penance for some horrid sin. We should be eternally challenging one another to the field and ten to one she beats me there. Or if I should I escape, she would kill me drinking.

RANTER: Here's a rogue! Your country should abound in such ladies!

DARING: The lord forbid! Half-a-dozen would ruin the land, debauch all the men and scandalize all the women.

SURELOVE: No matter. She's rich.

DARING: Ay, that will make her insolent.

SURELOVE: Nay, she's generous too.

DARING: Yes, when she's drunk. And then she'll lavish all.

RANTER: A pox on him! How he vexes me!

DARING: Then such a tongue! She'll rail and smoke till she choke again. And six gallons of punch hardly recovers her, and never but then is she good natured.

RANTER: I must lay him on!

DARING: There's not a blockhead in the country that's not …

RANTER: What?

DARING: Been drunk with her.

RANTER: I thought you meant something else, sir.

DARING: Nay, as for that, I suppose there is not great difficulty.

RANTER: 'Sdeath sir! You lie and you are a son of a whore! [*She draws and fences with him and he runs back round the stage.*]

DARING: Hold — hold, Virago — dear Widow, hold and give me thy hand.

RANTER: Widow!

DARING: 'Sdeath! I knew thee by instinct, Widow, though I seemed not to do so, in revenge for the trick you put on me in telling me a lady died for me.

RANTER: Why such a one there is, perhaps as may dwindle forty or fifty years or so, but will never be her own woman again. That's certain.

DARING: Widow, I have a shrewd suspicion that you yourself may be this dying lady.

RANTER: Why so, coxcomb?

DARING: Because you took such pains to put yourself in my hands.

RANTER: Gad, if your heart were half so true as your guess, we might make a treaty of peace.

DARING: Give my thy hand, Widow. I am thine, and so entirely, I will never be drunk … outside of thy company. Prithee, let's go and bind the bargain.

RANTER: Nay faith, let's see the wars at an end first.

DARING: Nay prithee, take me in the humour while thy breeches are on for I never liked thee half so well in petticoats.

RANTER: Lead on, General. You give me good encouragement to wear them. [*They both remove their hats.*]

BETTY: Bill, you rascal, I hardly knew you. Bill?

[APHRA *turns and removes her mask.*]

BETTY: Why Aphra! Is it really you?

MARY: You're on, Betty.

BETTY: I'll do you proud. I will! The widow will LIVE!

MARY: Who are you talking to? [BETTY *and* MARY *move off.* APHRA *exits. Stage darkens.* MARY *strikes a match and lights a candle and becomes* MORALITY WOMAN.]

WOMAN: She did do Aphra proud. But to no avail, thank God. It was only fitting that the widow should die a quick and unqualified death. She did not survive the performance and, as far as I know, has never been revived. What we've done is to show you what a blustering, boisterous mistake she was. After all, a woman who is hardy, bold, passionate, aggressive is a contradiction in terms, do you not think? [*While* MARY *is speaking,* BETTY *also lights a candle and assumes the role of* MORALITY MAN.]

MAN: Betty Currer didn't survive either. The Widow Ranter was her last role. Not much was heard of her afterwards.

WOMAN: I suppose she found herself a protector or an accommodating husband.

MAN: And what of our fair couple? We who have done so much to rid you of such misshapen creations as Mistress Behn and her works.

WOMAN: Why, we live on.

MAN: We will always be with you. Come. Take one last journey with us. [MAN *comes forward with candle and holds it up.* WOMAN *does the same. They look about them.*]

WOMAN: Where are we?

MAN: Westminster Abbey. This is Poets' Corner. We are very fortunate to be here on this particular night. Look. See over there? [*Looks into audience.*]

WOMAN: No. Yes! Yes, I do. Figures. Dozens of them. Are they ghosts?

MAN: Yes. The ghosts of the bards whose remains are buried here. This is the night that new candidates are accepted into their midst.

WOMAN: So many of them! Who's that?

MAN: Shadwell.

WOMAN: Really!

MAN: And that's Jonson.

WOMAN: Samuel? He's lost weight.

MAN: Ben! And look! That balding fellow with the ruff.

WOMAN: This is wonderful!

MAN: And there's Chaucer ... Dryden ... Otway ... Lee ... Congreve ... Addison ... Gay ... Oh, now this will interest you. Observe that lady.

[*The figure of* APHRA, *also with a candle, emerges from the shadows.*]

WOMAN: That one? Dressed in the loose *robe de chambre* with her neck and breast bare.

MAN: [*Appreciatively*] Yes! How much fire in her eye! What a passionate expression in her motions, and how much assurance in her features!

WOMAN: Look, she's going up to Chaucer.

MAN: He's the president of the assembly.

WOMAN: He's saying something to her. She's giving him a really sour look. What's he saying?

MAN: He's telling her that none of her sex has any right to a seat there.

WOMAN: I should think not!

MAN: Look, she throws her eyes about to see if she can find any one who inclines to take her part.

WOMAN: [*Looking out to the audience*] Not one stirs. They're shaking their heads. [APHRA *flings out of the assembly, passing the two observers.*]

WOMAN: Wait, Madam, I would talk with you.

APHRA: Men! I dare say, I know of none that write at such a formidable rate but that a woman may well hope to reach their greatest heights.

WOMAN: The cheek!

APHRA: Peckerheads! [*She moves on.*]

WOMAN: How vulgar! Who is she? [*Light concentrates in a glowing way on the distorted faces of the* MORAL MONSTER. *They blow out their candles.* APHRA *turns and addresses the audience, an epistle from the grave.*]

> I will not wear your richly tattered cloak
> I discard your taboo skirt
> fashionable silence
> fear of all I ask for
> only what is fair
> a simple testament to the dignity of my labour
> all the joy of what I would not fear
> the love of kings, of whores, of drunkards
> of stars
> the universe of my fingertips
> my stubborn destiny
> everything
> in your face
> the laughter
> the dance
> the sex

the unmistakable success
I make no excuse
the fire of my wit
stands
the glory of what can't be denied
you who omit me
a full third night
and the promise of my Fame.

[*Lights fade slowly to black*]

About Aphra Behn [1640 – 1689]

Aphra Behn had travelled to the Americas, spied for King Charles the Second and spent time in debtors' prison all by the age of 30. In 1670, the production of her play *The Forced Marriage* launched her as a playwright and the first English woman writer to earn a living solely through her pen.

The Forced Marriage introduced a major theme in her work — that marriage for socio-economic reasons, in the interests of a stable society, was immoral. Aphra Behn believed that love for women as well as men should be free, unhampered by convention or control of any sort.

Seventeen of her plays were produced in her lifetime, mostly bawdy comedies that scandalized the audiences of the day. All were well crafted, entertaining, filled with memorable characters and wonderfully stageable. In addition to playwrighting, she wrote poetry and a number of novels that preceded Dafoe, usually considered the first English novelist, by nearly half a century.

Aphra Behn was an individualist in her writing and her life who challenged the popular expectations placed upon seventeenth-century women. After her death, moral opinion deemed that such a strong and "outrageous" voice coming from a woman should be silenced; her work was driven into oblivion and even her very existence denied.

APHRA is meant to be an introduction to the individual and the writer. While many of her own words and scenes have been incorporated into the play, *APHRA* is an interpretive picture, not a definitive one. We hope it will spur interest in her life and works.

About the Playwrights

Nancy Jo Cullen is a playwright, poet and fiction writer. Her plays *The Waitresses* (co-written with Anne Loree), *Forever There* and *Gone Tomorrow* (co-written with Rose Scollard) and *Another Saturday Night* were all produced by Maenad Theatre in Calgary, of which she was a co-founder. She has published three poetry books with Frontenac House: *Science Fiction Saint,* which was shortlisted for three awards (Best Alberta Trade book, Best Alberta Poetry Book and The Gerald Lampert Award); *Pearl* (which won the Best Alberta Trade Book award) and *Untitled Child.*

She is a graduate of the University of Guelph Humber MFA program and is the 4th recipient of the Writers' Trust Dayne Ogilvie Prize for LGBT Emerging Writer. Her fiction has appeared in *The Puritan, Grain, filling Station, Plenitude, Prairie Fire* and *This Magazine.* Two of her short stories were included in *The Journey Prize Anthology,* in 2012 and in 2014. Her short story collection, *Canary,* is the winner of the 2012 Metcalf Rooke Award. *Canary* published by Biblioasis in 2013, was highly acclaimed by reviewers across Canada.

She is at work on a novel and another collection of short stories.

Alexandria Patience is a writer, theatre director and performer. She was a founding member and Artistic Director of Maenad Theatre. She has written or contributed to *Mother Tongue, Aphra, The Cocoa Diary, Speaking in Mother Tongues* and *You.* A section from *You* was translated into Spanish and published in the Argentinian anthology *El Perfecto Sexo.* She was a founding member of the visual and performing arts group *MasQuirx,* which toured internationally. For many years Alexandria programmed for herland, a feminist film and video Celebration. Working with the homeless to give them a voice she created the video *see me,* which was screened at *Document 2* film festival in Glasgow and is used as a Scottish medical training tool. Recent audio art works include: two outdoor audio walks, *Portskerra/ Melvich Stories 1 & 2; DownloadLowdown,* a national podcast project in which she represented the North, the Hebrides, Orkney Islands and the Shetlands; and *Fichead Eun, a Children's Parliament* audio and visual art project in the Uists district of Scotland. She creates large-scale public art projects and has exhibited art works internationally. She is currently living on the north coast of Scotland and working as a freelance interdisciplinary artist and storyteller who also creates festivals and community events. Alexandria's core drive is the art of storytelling and a consuming interest in the rituals supporting us through death and grief.

Rose Scollard, another founder of Maenad Theatre, wrote *Metamorphoses I & II,* Maenad's first production. Three other of her plays — *Bete Blanche/Tango Noir, 13th God,* and *Shea of the White Hands* — also premiered with Maenad. During her time as Markin-Flanagan Distinguished Writers playwright-in-residence (1997) her play *Caves of Fancy,* about Mary Shelley and the creation of *Frankenstein,* was presented at the University of Calgary's international Shelley/Wollstonecraft conference and published in *Mary Wollstonecraft and Mary Shelley: Writing Lives* (Wilfrid Laurier University Press).

Fifteen of her plays have been collected electronically in *North American Women's Drama,* Alexander Street Press. *Firebird,* a play for young audiences, was translated into German as *Feuervogel* and premiered with Frie Kammerspiele in Magdeburg, Germany (2003). *Tango Noir,* a collection of three of her plays, was published by Frontenac House (2012). She is co-author with Caroline Russell-King of *Strategies: The Business of Being a Playwright in Canada,* (Playwrights Union of Canada, 2000).

Among her theatre awards are the CBC Write For Radio Prize for *The Man Who Collected Women* (1988) and Alberta Culture Playwriting Competition prizes for *Uneasy Pieces* and *Nosey Parkers* (1985). *Shea of the White Hands* was a finalist for the Susan Smith Blackburn Prize (1995). Her play *I Ain't so Tough* will be produced by Urban Stories in Calgary 2016.

About Maenad Theatre

Maenads were an ancient order of women who held wild ceremonies in honour of Dionysus. Today Dionysus is chiefly remembered as the god of wine, but in ancient times he was equally honoured as the god of theatre.

The connection between Maenads and theatre is scarcely ever drawn. Traditionally they had a reputation for running wild and tearing things apart, but their sacred mountain dancing and their song of worship, the dithyramb, were the foundations of Greek theatre.

Maenad Theatre was formed in Calgary by Alexandria Patience, Nancy Jo Cullen and Rose Scollard with the purpose of taking shows to fringe festivals. Sandra McNeill, and Brenda Anderson, both of whom directed Maenad shows were closely involved in those formative years. In 1989 Maenad was incorporated as a non-profit organization with the mandate to promote new and dynamic woman-centred works for theatre. Maenad believed that self-empowerment comes through self-production.

Our years with the Maenad theatre collective were marked by intensity, high spirits and the serendipitous way that gifted people always seemed to pop up when needed to bring our scripts to life. It is chiefly owing to their generous and inspired contributions to our productions that our plays were able to have a life on the stage. Our thanks to all those actors, choreographers, designers, directors, front of house volunteers, musicians, stage managers and crew, board members and countless others who worked for virtually nothing to create wonderful stage moments that shimmered for a while but still endure in memory.

Writing *Aphra*

In 1990 we decided to write a play about Aphra Behn. It was Nancy's idea and she didn't have much trouble persuading the rest of us. She had first heard of Behn in the early 80s from her Theatre History teacher, Jim Hoffman, at David Thompson University Centre. "He mentioned her in passing as the first woman playwright to make her living solely from her pen." We were at the time very involved with Maenad Theatre, which we had co-founded a few years earlier, and since our mandate as a theatre company was to promote the feminine vision through new works for theatre, a play about Aphra Behn seemed like the perfect project.

The first thing we did was read everything we could get our hands on. The University of Calgary library had a six-volume collection of Behn's plays that had been edited and published by Montague Summers in 1915. Summers, who at the time was chiefly known for his works on the occult, was also a respected scholar of 17th-century drama. His publication was the beginning of the resurrection of Aphra Behn and her plays and her return to the public consciousness again.

We read George Woodcock's *The Incomparable Aphra* (later published as *Aphra Behn: The English Sappho*), a generous and lively treatment of Behn. Woodcock saw her as an early anarchist and as an important influence on the development of the English novel.

We felt Victoria Sackville West's *Aphra Behn: the Incomparable Astrea* was not a sympathetic book. West conceded that she rather liked Behn but felt that she'd wasted her gifts as a writer; that she had only one theme — sex; and that her writing was superficial. She also noted that Behn had "made a few astute observations, of a rather vulgar kind; that she had a supply of quick and easy dialogue, and that much vaunted management of situation: this constitutes her stock in trade." Rose would like to say here that as someone who has struggled with the dramatic form for some years she personally would kill for Aphra Behn's stock in trade. Her theatrical capability may seem easy as she executes it but it definitely is not easy to acquire.

I'm glad to say we found a strong counter-argument to Sackville West's point of view in a very well researched and elegantly written dissertation by Tom Lasswell: *Two plays of Aphra Behn: The Rover Part 1 and The Feigned Curtezans. A Theatrical Defence of the Author and the Comedy of Intrigue.* Arguing that many of the scholars who have written on Aphra have had no practical experience in the theatre and thus have missed much of her artistry, he analyses in great detail her mastery of the dramatic and comedic art.

After steeping ourselves in all these materials the overriding impression that we shared was that Behn had been a dynamite personality with a very exciting life. Although very few of the claims about her life have been verified, for us a very clear image of an energetic and "happening" personality shone through the vague and gossipy speculations of history. Here was a woman who had most probably travelled to the Americas, had married and been widowed, spied for King Charles the Second in the Netherlands and had spent time in debtor's prison, all by the age of 30. In the next twenty years she turned to theatre and in that time the London stage was rarely without one of the comedies that sealed her success as a playwright.

The Cavalier Restoration was a major factor in her story. England was coming out of a long period of cultural drought that the Puritans had imposed. There was a general loosening of restrictions. Women were allowed for the first time on the English stage as actors. There was an overall openness and an anything-goes attitude in society. Even so, Aphra was criticized for her outspokenness and her unconventional views. And she came close to imprisonment for them. We decided that we wanted to include some of the features of Aphra's life in our play.

Our second discovery was that Mrs. Behn was a very good playwright, and for this, thanks to Montague Summers, we didn't have to rely on supposition but good hard copy. As we read her plays we were amazed by the quantity of work and by the quality as well. She was a writer comfortable in her craft. She wrote seventeen or more plays, mostly bawdy comedies that scandalized and delighted the London theatre-going world. Her plays were notable for the numerous roles for women — women who were clearly in charge of their lives.

Aphra Behn died at the age of fifty, and almost before she was buried the rumour mills started. She became in the eighteenth and nineteenth centuries the symbol of bawdiness and pornographic writing. She was seen as an "unclean fiend," and her works were thought to be so indecent they were unreadable. Few people actually read the work to see if this was true or not. They just inferred that if her reputation was that bad her work must be as well. She was condemned without trial and, apart from the odd pot shot by self-righteous critics, for the next 225 years remained in oblivion until Montague Summers single-handedly brought her back into the playing field.

This silencing of Aphra Behn really shocked us. That wonderful lively joyful voice just snuffed out. Somehow or other we wanted to register that shock in our play.

Our first decision about *Aphra* was that it would be a play with three women in it. We didn't know it at the time but another play was being written about Aphra by Toronto playwright Beth Hurst, which was to focus on her love life. It was called *A Woman's Comedy*. What we wanted to focus on we didn't quite know at this point — we just knew that it would have a triad of women in it. Perhaps they would portray the three mythical stages of her life: virgin, matron, crone.

We did a lot of exercises. Freefall. Brainstorming. We'd go away and write. We'd come back together and write. We did this before we got the main plot of the play and we did it afterwards as well.

During this inventive time we came up with a concept that interested us and helped structure the play — the idea of a two-fold monster, Moral Man and Moral Woman, representing the societal forces that worked against Aphra during her lifetime, gathered strength as she was dying, and totally wiped her off the slate after her death.

By this time we had found out enough about Aphra's theatrical life to know that most of the best women actors of her day had performed in her plays, including the King's mistress Nell Gwyn. We toyed with the idea of using Nell but in the end chose two other actors, Mary Betterton, a demure and gentle woman, the wife of producer Tom Betterton; and Betty Currer, a high-spirited, flashy performer who loved wicked and saucy roles. Aphra herself would complete the triad, and the morality monster would be played by the same actors who played Mary and Betty.

Another vivid image that came up in our writing exercises was the idea of Aphra in the delirium of her last hours hallucinating that she was breaking out in paper cuts. We just loved that paper cut image and we played around with it a lot and finally incorporated it into the play.

At this point we still didn't have a story. Then we got lucky. We actually found a letter that stated that Aphra's last play, produced posthumously, had been deliberately mangled in the theatre. There seemed little doubt that the play — The Widow Ranter — was condemned because of the brash and unladylike character of the eponymous Widow. We decided that this suppression of The Widow Ranter would be the subject of our play.

We had spent a number of months reading and researching; now we settled down to the writing of the play. We decided to set the story a day or two before Aphra's death. She is writing strenuously, putting the final polish to *The Widow Ranter*, but she is desperately ill and her friends Mary Betterton and Betty Currer have come to nurse her and cheer her up. Part of the cheering up is their promise to produce *The Widow Ranter*.

The Widow is a smoking, drinking, brawling woman who is madly in love with Colonel Daring. She puts on britches and challenges him to a duel and wins his heart. Betty is dying to play the role of Ranter. Mary is a bit more demure and a bit more realistic. She is sure, and so is her producer husband, that the public will reject the Widow. But Aphra is so ill and so wretched they make the promise anyway, not at all sure that it will be kept.

In the second half of the play, Aphra, now dead, returns to see the production of *The Widow Ranter* at the Duke's Theatre, only to find that the producers have done everything in their power to kill the play. Betty, who is finally realizing her dream to play the Widow, is outraged at the way the producers have mishandled it. "The play doesn't have a chance," she fumes. "The best play that was ever writ wouldn't have a chance, if it had the fate to be murdered like this. The casting is lamentable, the acting execrable. Here I am about to play this torrid scene with *Samuel Sanford*. A man better suited to playing Caliban. He's round shouldered, meagre faced, spindle-shanked, splay footed. It's the worst casting job in the history of the Duke's." These lines were based on the aforementioned letter in which the writer concluded that a hatchet job had been done on the play so that it would not succeed.

We decided to include as much as we could of Aphra's own writing in the play. And so we put a scene from *The Widow Ranter* in each act. We also found another scene which worked very well with our story: the Doctor Scene from *Sir Patient Fancy*. It's a crazy madcap putdown of medical quackery and worked very well with our treatment of Aphra's delirium. Excerpts from some of Behn's letters and prologues were also incorporated, and our last scene was created with the help of an article about her written in the 19th century.

So that might give you an idea of how our collective writing process worked. The play was staged in 1991, a lush costume drama that we felt made a rich and ornate frame for our newly constructed portrait of the first English playwright to earn a living by her pen.

Maenadic Rites on Stage

Susan Stone-Blackburn, a Professor of English and former Dean of Graduate Studies at the University of Calgary, conducted the following interview at the time we were producing Aphra. *We've included it here because we feel it calls up the energy and vitality we experienced as part of Maenad.*

The Maenad Theatre Company is a collective that started with Fringe productions in Edmonton in the summers of 1987 and 1988. They incorporated in 1989 and have completed two seasons at Calgary's Pumphouse Theatre. The three women at Maenad's artistic core are playwright Rose Scollard, poet-playwright and actress Nancy Cullen, and Alexandria Patience, director and actress, who has recently added playwriting to her repertoire. All the Maenad productions have been new Canadian plays written, directed and, for the most part, designed by women: the company mandate is "to promote the feminine vision through exciting and dynamic new works for the theatre."

The rapidly developing company is entering a new phase with its 1991-92 season which will see an expansion of the collective, two plays authored or co-authored by women new to the group, and a remounting of Cullen's, Patience's and Scollard's play about 17th century playwright Aphra Behn. *Aphra* will be presented in conjunction with "Breaking the Surface," an interactive festival/conference of women, theatre and social action that Maenad is co-hosting with the University of Calgary's Department of Drama from 13-17 November 1991.

Reflecting their commitment to a collaborative mode, the interview on 11 June 1991 brought Patience, Scollard and Cullen together around Scollard's dining room table, the site of much collective thinking.

Stone-Blackburn: You've completed two seasons and you have exciting plans for the next, so Maenad is looking less like a hopeful experiment and more like a company with a future. What has worked for you?

Scollard: I think it's creative energy that's propelled us through two years of really hard work on a tight budget. We've had a shared vision.

Patience: We started from a feeling of a void, with no company in town or in the vicinity that could produce the type of theatre we found very exciting. There's a lack of a female vision in mainstream theatre and even in a lot of experimental theatre.

Cullen: I just finished reading *Fair Play*, interviews of Canadian women playwrights. So many of them felt that a woman's point of view isn't seen as valid by traditional theatrical hierarchies. We felt a kind of general misunderstanding of our consciousness, a discrediting of it.

Patience: As an actress, there's a potential for boredom in the roles you have to perform — they can be very superficial adjuncts to the story. It's not that there aren't strong roles for women, but not enough. There's a lot of excitement and strength in initiating, taking the power, saying "we can do it."

Stone-Blackburn: Maenad's stated mandate is "to promote the feminine vision." How does that differ in your minds from *feminist* vision?

Cullen: I think you see a group of different kinds of feminists at this table. But the word "feminist" means so many things. It's a very loaded word. We might as well have said we were feminists because critics jump quickly from "feminine" to "feminist." It's because we don't want to be labelled that we stayed away from the word. At the time we incorporated it seemed to mean a certain kind of theatre. I think I've changed my views on that, but some of us haven't, so as a company, "feminine" is still the best word for us.

Scollard: I think I'm a feminist the same way I'm an atheist, but I don't want that to be the label on my life. I don't want to be mentally or spiritually limited by the label, even though I would fight to the death for certain feminist causes. We want to include a great many other things besides feminism — we want to give women a voice, and not all women are voicing feminist concerns. They want to talk about their Jungian approach to things or… .

Cullen: But we are still looking for an *alternative* female view, don't you think? Somebody who's trying to draw a new map for herself is what I see in a lot of women's theatre. Maybe, in retrospect, we should have said we do a "woman-centred theatre." Maybe "feminine" is loaded too — the opposite of "feminist."

Patience: I agree with Rose and Nancy on the focus being wider than what would be considered feminist. As Rose said, if you're a feminist, if you're an atheist — if you're a vegetarian — those things tend to be in your writing because they're you. Part of the reason we went for "feminine" was that we also were looking at incorporating the feminine side of a masculine person, as opposed to just pure feminist. The truth of it is that we've produced just pieces by women because that's the voice we feel is being left behind and needs to be drawn forward. I still think that "feminine" vision is something we're struggling for, and I like the struggle.

Scollard: Actually, our real mandate as "Maenads" was to promote the orgiastic and visionary concerns of women. We changed the bylaws and took out "Orgiastic" because everybody said no one will ever give you funding!

Cullen: Now we've realized that we really didn't want to get into that whole funding thing.

Patience: Our productions are very lush, very sexy.

Scollard: Orgiastic, not just as a sexual term but as a ritualistic one.

Patience: And celebratory.

Cullen: A Maenadic ritual was an orgiastic ritual.

Patience: We struck it from our bylaws, but we carry it in our hearts. And I think that's what really affects our work, that kind of celebratory, ritualistic, sexual aspect of ourselves. It doesn't necessarily come out as sexuality is commonly perceived — some of it is choreography or the lighting — maybe not "sexual," but "sensual" is a better word.

Stone-Blackburn: How did you get started?

Scollard: Our first show was *Metamorphoses I and II*, two short plays with Alexandria and Barbara Campbell Brown and John Paulsen, directed by Sandra McNeill. It was a wonderful little group of people for our first experience in self-production, very exciting to see it come to life. One of the plays was picked up by CBC's *Vanishing Point*.

Cullen: I co-wrote *The Waitresses* with singer-songwriter Ann Loree in Mexico. Somebody told us this woman named Alexandria Patience would probably direct it. She read the script and said she would. We scrambled to produce this little rock musical for The Fringe in Edmonton. Alex asked me to stage manage my play and also Rose's *Tango Noir*, so that's how I met Rose and Alex.

Scollard: That summer was a tough summer for me [1988] because my father died, and *Tango Noir* just went on without me. It was so astonishing to come back and see a group of people just making it happen, and everything about it was so beautiful, I was just mesmerized by the production. Nancy was toiling away painting chairs and I thought, "Wow! Why is she doing all this?"

Patience: (*She laughs.*) Because her play wasn't going to happen otherwise.

Scollard: It just seemed like a miracle to me. I didn't see it at either the Edmonton or Vancouver Fringes, so I phoned the

Pumphouse Theatre, and we arranged to put it on in Calgary. We got such favourable reviews, we thought maybe we could make it as a real theatre company. Nancy was writing *Forever There* and I had *Thirteenth God* written and a children's play, *Firebird,* in the works, and that was our season. Our opener, *Thirteenth God*, had music, choreography, incredible sets, masks, everything. I was happy with every aspect of that Calgary production.

Cullen: We did *Forever There* in the Pumphouse's small theatre, the Joyce Doolittle Theatre, where we'd done *Tango Noir*. I think what we learned in that production was how much we loved that space.

When we brought Kathleen Foreman in to direct, we discussed at the outset how we thought a production would work and the kind of interaction we hoped to encourage between all members of the production. It worked very well and gave us a bond with Kathleen that has gone on.

Scollard: With *Firebird*, though we said we wouldn't, we somehow got back into a major production in the Pumphouse's big theatre. The results were really beautiful, but the amount of work really did underline for us that we weren't equipped to do major productions like that more than once every ten years. But we had a wonderful designer, Heather Kent, and Geoffrey Gerwing's masks were incredible.

Patience: It was a big set, even on a small budget. We've had a lot of support from Calgary's theatre community. Every company in town has helped us — with rehearsal space, set-building space, costumes rented for next to nothing, everything. We scavenged from JV's production company. What Heather wanted from us was the opportunity to create a set and have control, so we let her. We paid the price in hard work! But if we weren't willing to do something that allowed her that freedom, she really wasn't interested. And she was the driving force that made it happen. *Firebird* felt the way it did because of how it looked. It was a magical piece that really called for the set it had.

Cullen: So the next show was small and cheap! We opened our second season with a one-woman show, *Gone Tomorrow*.
Scollard: Nancy and I had decided almost at the same time we wanted to try monologues. I wrote one play and Nancy wrote two, and we brought them back and they fitted together. It was just amazing on Alex's first read-through how many parallels there were in ideas.

Patience: At that point we were saying that the design would grow out of the piece, that instead of having a designer, the collective process would be used to pull the design together, so Elisa Filipetto (the stage manager) and Charlotte Lee (the director) and I sat around after one rehearsal and talked about what we needed, and then we designed it … . That central piece of Rose's has since been produced as a radio play with myself again doing the part of Rachel.

Cullen: And then we did [*all in chorus*] *Aphra*. We wrote it collaboratively, all three of us. We spent a long time around the table deciding how we were going to do it, reading and sharing what we'd read, discussing what we'd write, and keeping the actual theatre space in mind, creating for that space.

Scollard: One of our goals was not only to use the smaller space to work within very stringent budgets, but also to explore that space, and with *Aphra* we really met that goal thoroughly for the first time. That was largely due to Alex's direction, I would say, and Sandi Somers's design.

Patience: A friend let me know that the Calgary Opera was clearing their storage space, so I went and scammed all kinds of stuff that went into making our next set. It was really fortuitous — that huge frame, the chaise longue — which is now in my living room, even the drapes and groundcloth: all free!

Cullen: Lizzie Wattie did a lot of great work on costumes as well, and Sandi helped incorporate all of that in the design and did some absolutely stunning lighting.

Patience: I'm not sure another designer could have dealt with coming in on a Sunday having seen only different pieces not in context — it was like a picture puzzle. She was willing to fly by the seat of her pants, and we trusted her to make it work ... . We finished the season with *Bête Blanche/Tango Noir* directed by Gerri Hemphill — with another excellent design by Sandi.

Stone-Blackburn: What do you see as your biggest success?

Scollard: *Aphra* has been the most successful, because our audience was very comfortable with what we tried to do in retrieving a woman from the garbage heap. [Aphra Behn plunged into obscurity after her death, despite great success as a playwright in the late seventeenth century.] We showed a woman who'd been silenced and brought back her voice.

Cullen: In a way, she's Everywoman.

Scollard: We've had a lot of interest in that play, a lot of excitement from a wider range of people than we expected. But in some of our other plays, right or wrong isn't so clearly defined from a feminist viewpoint and they're not so easy to label. Sometimes we're critical of women.

Patience: Like *Bête Blanche/Tango Noir* really is a cautionary tale. In *Bête Blanche*, the woman is in a fantasy world, basically cutting all the lines to reality, and by the time she comes to realize it, it's too late. That could be viewed as not supporting a feminist perspective of women. But these are seductions that we all feel to a greater or lesser extent.

Stone-Blackburn: And that's not your only play about a woman being seduced by her fantasy.

Cullen: No, *Forever There* is a media fantasy, the romance, coming to life in a woman's living room. I think the response to that was fairly good, though the ending disturbed a lot of people.

Stone-Blackburn: Not definite enough?

Cullen: I think that's what it was. Both newspaper reviewers felt that I hadn't made a clear enough statement about whether Harlequins were good or bad. They couldn't deal with my treatment of Grace, who was just left hanging. It is the same theme — a woman is seduced by her fantasies until she's left with nothing. Those plays are really dark, sinister in a lot of ways.

Scollard: In the case of *Bête Blanche*, some people felt that by making Faye responsible for her own corruption, I was somehow letting women down, and that Faye, in fact, was a victim of her circumstances — being in the Depression, being poor and having a weak husband made her what she was.

Patience: But that was their choice to decide that. I don't understand why people feel that we should stamp theatre — because they perceive us as political theatre, and I think we are — so that it's rigid, clear-cut, and there's nothing to be interpreted. Theatre is an interactive experience. The audience has to come with their perspective and see where the play connects with them in their lives.

Stone-Blackburn: You've been talking about audience responses — what about your own ideas about what constitutes success?

Cullen: I see personal success in terms of what I've learned from each piece; it's helped me to solidify a vision of where I see my work in theatre going. In a sense, success for me is a real belief in myself and confidence in the validity of my work. Since we started I've become stronger and able to cope with the reality of making theatre from a female point of view.

Scollard: I think for me success lies in learning to trust the process — it gets better every time, and somehow or other you pull it out of the hat every time, and it's just amazing to me that that happens. We've had wonderful people to work with;

they all seem to be getting better at the process too. I've moved from a position of worrying about whether I'll ever be produced to learning to trust what I want to do. I don't think I'm any more in a position to be produced in traditional theatres than I was; I haven't "progressed" in that respect, but I now respect the separation [between "small" theatres and mainstream ones].

Stone-Blackburn: What's been the hardest for you?

Cullen, Patience and **Scollard:** [*in chorus*] Working collaboratively.

Patience: It's an ongoing, very, very difficult process. You kind of have to feel it — you can discuss what the collaborative process is, but when it actually comes down to doing it and producing theatre, you can only do that by doing it.

Cullen: Communication, understanding … each time you get a new person, you have to start inventing the wheel again. And each time we do a new project, we tend to have new people in the cast or the production crew. Our core is pretty solid, but we keep changing, and some people are better at collaboration than others.

Patience: Each person defines what her contribution and her connection with Maenad will be.

Scollard: We want to include a wider group of people in Maenad but it's very difficult to move out of the triad we've formed. It's a very strong triad, and because there's always so much work to do immediately, we've been consumed with doing that, and communication with other members of the group has always been a weak point.

Patience: We've just started having monthly meetings — the third part in the process. The first part was Nancy, Rose and I just getting the show up at any cost. The second was the three of us gathered around this table here, saying "Well, what do we want for next year? What are our personal ambitions?" It was the personal drives of the three of us that made last season happen. This is the third part of the process, trying to open up. We're trying to define how we can work with a larger group and still manage to survive. We're on the cutting edge between chaos and ... (*laughs*) anarchy.

Stone-Blackburn: Maenad is shaped to a large extent by writers engaged in self production, but I've been really impressed by the theatrical creativity in your productions. Maenad seems to have writers who are unusually able at stagecraft. You seem very fluid in contributions.

Cullen: I think that's the collective. We've established a trust between the three of us. But there's also something specifically female about it — I know Rose disagrees. I'm not saying that men can't work this way, it's just that women's concepts of power are different. We train each other how to take power, how to share power.

Scollard: I think women are comfortable in the collaborative process, but I don't care to think that collaboration is the exclusive domain of women. Essentially theatre is a collaborative process. Because we don't have any money, we're exploring, that's why our plays are theatrical. I've learned a lot from watching Alexandria direct, and of course it is the collaboration — everybody has something creative to bring to it, and the more you allow those different abilities to work, the better it will be.

Patience: Also, there's a taste for theatricality. Theatricality is something we like, that Sandi Somers, who's designed a lot of our shows, likes — that lushness. When I see theatre, I want it different from film, different from television, so you have to work with the advantages theatre gives you, and part of that is creating an image that's as lush as possible. That's why I loved working on Aphra, the feeling of all that baroque.

Stone-Blackburn: Nancy, you've just been to the second International Women Playwrights Conference in Toronto. Did that give you some sense of how your experience compares with that of other playwrights?

Cullen: Absolutely. It made me see that women's work across the globe is marginalized. It's a frustration of all the writers that were there, that their work isn't taken seriously, that they struggle with validation, with having their voices heard. I thought, "Okay, I'm not isolated, we're all working towards the same thing, and if we all keep working on it, we won't be such a weird, marginal group." There are groups like Maenad springing up all over the place. It was quite inspirational to me, women from other countries who think that what we're doing is very interesting and exciting, and to realize once again that it is. I came back excited about doing new work.

Stone-Blackburn: What made you decide to change direction and look for other people's scripts for next year?

Cullen: We actually wanted to from the start. We had to prove ourselves, prove that it could work, before anybody else would want to get on board. To send out a call for submissions that said we're not paying you and we have no money, but if you're interested — and then to get such excellent submissions — was really inspiring.

Scollard: We set ourselves up as promoting the feminine vision. We never saw the feminine vision as being exclusively our property, but we didn't have a structure for considering other work. So when we decided to expand, the first thing we did was set up a structure. We didn't necessarily want to become a highly structured, organized company.

Patience: We're trying to keep the machine minimal so it doesn't overwhelm the creativity. It's a really precarious balance, one that almost every small company has to deal with.

Stone-Blackburn: So what will next season's plays be?

Scollard: We'll remount *Aphra* in conjunction with *Breaking the Surface* in November. It seems to suit the conference and it's something we can remount without a lot of initial angst. It's being published in *Theatrum* in September, so it might be a good time to remount it. The other two plays we chose by inviting submissions and have them juried by Nancy Cullen, Joyce Doolittle and Barbara Campbell Brown. The plays are *Gertrude and Ophelia* by Margaret Clarke and *Mother Tongue* by Cheryl L'Hirondelle and Alexandria Patience.

Cullen: Clarke's idea was so exciting, it just caught us. The playwright examines the story of Hamlet from the perspective of Gertrude and Ophelia. It's an excellent script, and it appealed to us as a very theatrical piece.

Scollard: It created a lot of excitement in the group. It was given a reading last night after a week's workshop. *Mother Tongue,* Alex can explain.

Patience: It's quite process-oriented. We don't have a single director; we're hoping to have lots of different "inspirational eyes" come in. Part of what they will be doing will be inspiration for Cheryl and me, working up a process of rehearsal in which the performer decides what pieces to put together and how to put them together, and make that process very visible for the audience. The theme we are going to explore is the naïve appropriation of culture. Cheryl is Metis and I am Scottish, and as an autobiographical fact, we actually naïvely appropriated the other's culture when we were children.

Stone-Blackburn: I share your excitement about the season; I look forward to it.

Production History, Maenad Theatre

A woman-centred theatre company producing
original works for theatre

1987-2000 MAENAD FACT SHEET

Our Mandate:

Maenad Theatre was a Calgary-based woman-centred company that promoted women's visions through exciting and dynamic new works for theatre. Maenad was interested in the artistic visions of women whose voices were seldom heard in mainstream theatre, especially women of colour, First Nations women, and women with disabilities. We were the only woman-centred theatre company west of Toronto that annually produced a season of new works. Maenad Theatre stopped producing in 2000 and all materials, scripts, production materials are now held in The Glenbow Museum, Calgary, Alberta.

Our Work:

The company was founded by Nancy Jo Cullen, Alexandria Patience and Rose Scollard. From the time it was formed in 1987, Maenad produced the following premieres of plays by women and provided strong roles for women on and off the stage that went against the usual stereotypes. Each Spring a jury selected from submitted proposals the full-length works to be presented in the upcoming season. New Voices/ Fem Fest proposals were sent specifically to the Artistic Director, Alexandria Patience.

- August, 1987: *Metamorphoses I & II* by Rose Scollard. A bizarre and very funny feminist duet consisting of two short plays, *The Chosen* and *Mandatory Tiger*. *The Chosen* was adapted as a radio play for CBC's Vanishing Point. Director: Sandra McNeill, cast: 2 women, 1 man.

- August, 1988: *Tango Noir* by Rose Scollard. Crossing gender and character, the French writer Colette and the famous courtesan and spy Mata Hari contend with their young lovers and their need to be the femme fatale. Director: Brenda Anderson; cast: 1 woman, 1 man.

- June, 1988: *The Waitresses* by Nancy Cullen and Anne Loree. A musical comedy based on the lives of three different styles of waitresses who are all looking for what is important to them. Director: Alexandria Patience; cast: 3 women plus 1 musician.

- June 14 – July 1, 1989: *13th God* by Rose Scollard. A many-layered view of women dealing with the sensual and sexual aspects of all ages of their lives during three different eras: ancient Greek at the time of the maenads, the Edwardian, and the present. This is the work that gave our company its name. Original music by Kevin Labchuk; director: Brenda Anderson; cast: 3 women, 3 men.

- October 19 – November 4, 1989: *Forever There* by Nancy Jo Cullen. An allegorical and comic exploration of the effects of escapist romance novels on Grace, home alone for the weekend when her dream self and dream lover arrive. Director: Kathleen Foreman; cast: 2 women, 1 man.

- June 2 – 18, 1990: *Firebird* by Rose Scollard. A feminist re-visioning of an old folk tale in which the Princess becomes the wolf and guides the Prince (with the aid of the old wise woman) to save Firebird. Director: Alexandria Patience; cast: 3 women, 2 men.

- October 4 – 20, 1990: *Gone Tomorrow* by Nancy Jo Cullen and Rose Scollard. Three monologues that explore three different women's stories. *Gone Tomorrow* was also produced by Kathleen Flaherty as a radio play for CBC. Director: Charlotte Lee; cast: 1 woman.

- May 1 – 18, 1991: *Bete Blanche/Tango Noir* by Rose Scollard. Companion pieces that inhabit shifting dreamscapes in which women gain self-knowledge. Original music by Kevin Labchuk; director: Gerri Hemphill; cast: 1 woman & 1 man.

- February 21 – March 16, 1991: *APHRA* by Nancy Jo Cullen, Alexandria Patience and Rose Scollard. The last intrigue of 17th-century playwright Aphra Behn, the first English-speaking woman to make her living as a writer. Published in Theatrum, September 1991; produced by City Theatre in Victoria in February 1992; director: Alexandria Patience; cast: 3 women.

- October 31 – November 16, 1991: *APHRA.* A remount of the spring production with Tanya Lukenoff replacing Nancy Jo Cullen in the title role.

- November 13 – 17, 1991: *Breaking the Surface.* An International Interactive Festival/Conference of Women, Theatre and Social Action, presenting performances by: Maenad Theatre, Omaha Magic Theater (USA), Sistren (Jamaica), Veena Sood (Vancouver), Company of Sirens (Toronto), Theatre Parminou (Victoriaville), Shawna Dempsey & Lorri Millan (Winnipeg); and *The First Cabaret,* hostessed by Jan Derbyshire, co-hosted with the Drama Department at the University of Calgary.

- January 30 – February 15, 1992: *Gertrude and Ophelia* by Margaret Clarke. A feminist revisioning of the women in

Hamlet with their version of the Hamlet saga. Published in Theatrum April/May 1993 and produced for the Edmonton Fringe in 1994. Director: Joyce Doolittle; cast: 2 women, 1 man.

- April 16 – May 2, 1992: *Mother Tongue* by Cheryl L'Hirondelle and Alexandria Patience. A performance work that explores and shares the similarities and differences of two performers and their art and cultures: Scottish and Metis. Inspirational Eyes: Mark Dicey, Leila Sujir & Michael Green; cast: 2 women and 1 musician. A concurrent *Mother Tongue* installation/exhibition and performance was held at Truck, an artist-run centre, Calgary.

- October 20 – November 7, 1992: *New Voices/Fem Fest.* Maenad's first annual festival to encourage new works by women included *Landlady and Tenant* by Jay Blue; *Mothers and Daughters* by JoAnne James and All Nations Theatre; *Down All My Days* by Pat Benedict; and *White Room* by Kysten Blair and performances by Cheryl Foggo, masQuirx, Cory Mack and Jeanne Rokosh. An accompanying *Cabaret* included Winnipeg-based performance collaborators Shawna Dempsey and Lorri Millan, British performance artist Alexa Wright, Japanese butoh performer Hiroko Tamano, musician/performer Gudrun Gut from Berlin with Canada's Myra Davies, Lori Weidenhammer (aka Zucchini Mama to the performance aware) from Saskatchewan, Ali Riley from Toronto, and Calgary's Leila Sujir, Jill Swartz, Alice Lee, and Nancy Jo Cullen with Joni Brent.

- December 5, 1992: *A Celebration of Feminist Video & Performance.* Daytime: A gathering of video artists and a sharing of work by and about women with Rita McKeough, Leila Sujir, Sandra Vida, and Colleen Kerr (all from Calgary), Meena Nanji (Los Angeles), Ruth Lounsbury, Marina Zurkow and Abigail Simon (New York), Sara Diamond (Banff), Shauna Beharry (Moose Jaw), Pauline Cummins (Ireland) and Gita Saxena and Ian Rashid

(Toronto). Night time: Multi-media performance of *Mary Medusa* by Shawna Dempsey & Lorri Millan.

- Feb 25 – Mar 13, 1993: *Bluto* by Jill Swartz. A dense multi-faceted view of the life of a woman living in a world with no moral coherence in which she struggles though personal affirmations of joy and love to find a sense of harmony. *Bluto* is Maenad's first chapbook. Director: Alexandria Patience; cast: 5 women plus 2 vocal and 2 musicians.

- April 29 – May 15, 1993: *Dance Me Born* by Alice Lee shows, by following the lives of a sister and brother who were separated in childhood, how the Metis and Native peoples heal themselves through story, ritual and dance. Directors: Robin Melting Tallow and Amethyst First Rider; cast: 4 women, 4 men plus 2 dancers and 1 drummer.

- June 23 – 26, 1993: *E. Pauline Johnson (Tekahionwake)* by Betty Donaldson. Based on the writings and life of Tekahionwake and performed on and at the shores of the Glenmore Reservoir with the audience travelling in canoes. Director: Jenny Paine; cast: 3 women, 1 man plus 1 singer.

- October 7 – 23, 1993: *Another Saturday Night* by Nancy Jo Cullen. A karaoke musical of homo & hetero love set in a woman's washroom during the wedding reception of 8 ½-month pregnant Kelsey, with Nurse Cherry Ames presiding as the good fairy at the celebrations. Director: Charlotte Lee; cast: 4 women and 2 men.

- November 30 – December 19, 1993: *New Voices/Fem Fest* included: *everything you always wanted to know about gender* by All Nations Theatre; *Summer Solstice: Roll over Strindberg* by Some Friends; *One Short Phone Call* by Kelly Daniels; *Calipers* by Carole Thorpe; *Egg* by Lucinda Neufeld; *Reclaim* by Michelle Thrush; *Rubber Neckin'* by Carmen Stockton; *Bone Deep* by Cynthia Wells; *Through My Eyes* by Mia Blackwell.

- *The December 1993 Cabaret:* Shawna Dempsey and Lorri Millan's *Mermaid In Love* and *The Feminist Rant*; *The Gorgon Sisters* by MasQuirx; performances by Suzette Mayr & Hiromi Goto; an all-women comedy improv team; and , as the finale, the all women band *maud*.

- March 10 – 26, 1994: *The Dolly Rockers* by Colleen Craig. It's 1974 and an all-women rock band tours across Canada trying to make it big and survive, while their hot lead guitarist deals with her sexuality. Director: Alexandria Patience; cast: 5 women plus 2 musicians.

- March, 1994: *Laudes Matris* by Marcia Epstein, the premiere of a liturgy for God the Mother. Performances for International Women's Day. Director: Dawn Johnson; cast: 25 women plus 5 dancers, 5 percussion.

- June 6 – 9, 1994: *Exposure One & Two*, a festival of performance by women: *Clit Notes* and *World Without End* by Holly Hughes; *Lies about Betty and the Truth about Zucchini* by Lori Weidenhammer; *dark diaspora in dub* by ahdri zhina mandiela; and performances by Molly Chisakaay, Suzette Mayr, Diane Kooch, Nancy Jo Cullen, Alexandria Patience and Springboard Dance Collective. The program also included a 2-day intensive writers/ performers workshop with Holly Hughes on autobiographical performance.

- October 13 – 29, 1994: *The Oldest Woman in the World* by Gisèle Villeneuve. Maddie is turning 100 with the century but there's a lot of life left in her, so don't try to put her in any kind of a box. Director: Gail Hanrahan; cast: 3 women, 1 man plus 3 dancers.

- February 23 – March 11, 1995: *Shea of the White Hands* by Rose Scollard. Split between Ireland during the 1970s and Canada in the 1990s this contemporary translation of the tragic Tristan & Isolde story brings all involved to face the truth of who they are and what they have done. *Shea of the*

White Hands was a finalist for the Susan Smith Blackburn international contest for excellence in women playwrights. Director: Alexandria Patience; cast: 3 women, 3 men plus 3 actor/musicians.

- May 16 – June 4, 1995: *New Voices/Fem Fest 95: Fall of the Pomegranate* by Mariette Sluyter; *A Safe Place* by Carolyn Day, *Round-a-Bout* by Linda Delaney; *S & M*; *Always a Bridesmaid* and *Oh, How I want to be a Sunshine Girl* by Dayna McLeod; *Eve's Perfect Apple* by Michelle Wong; *Digs* by All Nations; *Dog's Diary* by Pam Boyd and Laurie Montemurro; *Myopic* by Nancy Jo Cullen; and *Goldilocks* by K-PTEL Tales.

- *The 1995 CABARET:* Shawna Dempsey and Lorri Millan's *Growing up Suite 1 & 2* and *The Plastic Bride*; stand-up comedy by Elvira Kurt; and the all-female bands maud & GASP!!

- June 13 – 17, 1995: *Fem Fest Holdover: Eve's Perfect Apple* & *Fall of the Pomegranate* by Mariette Sluyter.

- Oct 13 – 28, 1995: *The Cocoa Diary* by Suzette Mayr, Nicole Mion, Alexandria Patience and Sandi Somers. Maintaining your integrity can be a funny balancing game when you have the ambition to make it BIG in Art or Business. Facilitator: Gail Hanrahan; cast: 4 women.

- Dec 1 – 2, 1995: *The Alternative Christmas Cabaret* with *Milk of Amnesia* and *Red Hot Chile Christmas* by Carmelita Tropicana; and performances by Myra Davies, Alanna Jones, Mariette Sluyter, Carmen Stockton, Laurie Montemurro and Nicole Mion. Also included was a workshop lead by Carmelita Tropicana on *Women, Performance & Comedy*.

- March 2, 1996: *Urban Tattoo* written and performed by Marie Humber Clements. The history of cultural apartheid in Canada through a visceral journey of escape — from the allure of the city and the small-town beautiful delusions of priests to the sensual wisdom of the nightclub fortune teller, every step is raining stars. Facilitators: Coral Larson Thew and Alexandria Patience. Cast: 1 woman plus musicians. Also included were workshops lead by Marie in *Writing for Performance*, creating integrative writing/performance techniques.

- March 8 – 23, 1996: *Now Look What You Made Me Do* by Marie Humber Clements. The invidious process of violence and domination by one you love can make it ambiguous as to how you can love them, but it doesn't necessarily kill that love. Women and men survive but sometimes, to make that possible, a part of you has to die. Director: Coral Larson Thew; cast: 2-5 women, 1 man and 1 musician/actor.

- April 30 – May 18, 1996: *New Voices/Fem Fest '96: The Big Shock* by Deborah Green: *Afterthoughts* by Carmen Stockton; *A Weight On Me* by Laurie Montemurro; *Here I Stand Ironing* by Mariette Sluyter; *Full Circle* by Judith Lee Hoffer; *Miasma: Stupid as a Rose* by Myra Davies & Gudrun Gut.

- February, 1997: *Motherhood, Madness and the State of the Universe* by Kim Renders. In this one-woman show a number of narratives revolve around reflections on the inevitable process whereby a mother re-creates with her own children the relationships she had with her parents. Inevitably, her autobiographical reflections cause her to relate to her children in ways she'd rather not, and are interwoven with the fairy-tale like presentation of Renders's own mother's childhood.

- February, 1997: *The Lesbian Love Story of Tonto & the Lone Rangers & other Stories* by Shawna Dempsey & Lorri Millan. As in the body of their work thus far, Dempsey and Millan employ stylized costume and a careful, deliberate choice of voices to deliver a funny, sometimes raucous performance/ analysis of the roles women play in history. The manner in which women subvert and re-invent those roles which are otherwise inadequate to the necessities they face becomes the celebratory narrative affirming the strength and vitality of women's lives.

- May – June, 1997: *New Voice/Fem Fest: The Balkan Express* by The Company of Sirens; *Explaining Cosmology to a Live Chicken & Explaining Cosmology to a Dead Salmon* by Colleen Kerr; *Naming Names* by Lindsay Burns; and *Speaking In (Mother) Tongues* by Alexandria Patience.

- July, 1997: *Speaking In (Mother) Tongues* by Alexandria Patience and *Urban Tattoo* by Marie Humber at *The Women & Text Conference,* Leeds, England.

- September, 1998: *Speaking In (Mother) Tongues* by Alexandria Patience, Director: Marie Clements at *Other Worlds, Other Texts, Other Questions;* Osnabrück, Germany. Also readings, cabaret M.C. and a week-long workshop, *Creating Performance.*

- December, 1998 – June, 2000: The Traveller Project a theatre drama and a television /video production on international development (with Mary Thompson). Director: Alexandria Patience.

Bibliography

Books:

Hengen, Shannon. *Comedy's Edge: Volume II* Playwrights Guild of Canada, www.playwrightsguild.ca. Interviews with Nancy Jo Cullen, Alexandria Patience, Rose Scollard and several other women connected with Maenad: Myra Davies, Carmen Stockton, Laurie Montemurro, Michele Wong, Mariette Sluyter.

Lasswell, Tom. *Two Plays of Aphra Behn: The Rover, Part 1 and The Feigned Curtezans. A Theatrical Defence of the Author and the Comedy of Intrigue.* University of Oregon, 1982.

Sackville West, Victoria. *Aphra Behn: The Incomparable Astrea.* New York: Viking Press, 1928.

Summers, Montague (ed). *The Works of Aphra Behn,* (6 volumes) London: W. Heinemann; Stratford-on Avon: A. H. Bullen, 1915.

Woodcock, George. *The Incomparable Aphra.* AMS Press Inc. 1948

Woodcock, George. *Aphra Behn: The English Sappho.* Black Rose Books; New edition of 1948 edition *The Incomparable Aphra* (April 1 1989), Montreal

Articles:

Bennett, Susan, and Alexandria Patience. "Bad Girls Looking for Money — Maenad Making Feminist Theatre in Alberta." *Canadian Theatre Review 8,* 2 Spring 1995: 10-13.

Copeland, Nancy. "Imagining Aphra, Reinventing a Female Subject." *Theatre Topics V4.* I2, 1994. 135-144. John Hopkins University Press.

Stone-Blackburn, Susan. "Maenadic Rites on Stage in Calgary." Interview with Nancy Jo Cullen, Alexandria Patience, Rose Scollard. *Canadian Theatre Review 69,* Winter 1991: 28-33.

Stone-Blackburn, Susan. "Aphra Behn and Contemporary Canadian Women Playwrights." A comparative study of Behn's situation as a woman playwright then and Canadian women playwrights 300 years later, attempting to gauge what progress, if any, had been made for women playwrights. Maenad and Aphra are central in the article. *Woman as Artist: papers in honour of Marsha Hanen.* Edited by Christine Mason Sutherland and Beverly Jean Rasporich. Calgary: University of Calgary Press, 1993.

Acknowledgements

There are so many to thank. Maenad and its productions would never have happened without the support of hundreds of committed theatre workers and volunteers. This is especially true of *Aphra*. We acknowledge with deeply felt appreciation all those who worked so hard to help us celebrate the bright and gifted spirit that was Aphra Behn.